A Summer Love

TAMELLA WHITE

ISBN 979-8-89485-506-6 (Paperback)
ISBN 979-8-89485-507-3 (Digital)

Covenant Books
11661 Hwy 707
Murrells Inlet, SC 29576
www.covenantbooks.com

Todd, without your love, this book wouldn't
be possible. And to our heavenly Father
who gave us strength through it all.

CHAPTER 1

IT WAS A DELICIOUS SUMMER day, and the fragrant smells of freshly bloomed flowers were in the air. As Caroline stood on the veranda, she looked longingly at the vast, green mountains in front of her estate and wondered when she would ever find her true love. For months she had walked out onto the veranda, the gentle breeze would blow her blonde hair across her face, and she would whisper a prayer, hoping that by some miracle the man of her dreams would somehow mysteriously appear.

Caroline was a widow; her husband had died from complications during surgery, and she was left alone to raise her two children, Sarah and John. Sarah was a beautiful, intelligent, young woman with wisdom beyond her years. She had such compassion and gentleness, yet she was strong and cou-rageous, and it was her dream to become a teacher. Sarah had worked hard in school and won a pres-tigious scholarship to attend the ladies' college in Boston. She so much wanted to follow in her mother's footsteps.

John was a very handsome, bright, young man. He hoped to become an architect. He was a very talented artist in building models. John would sit for hours working on his sketches and models. However, John had always been a sickly child and was unable to attend school when he was young because of the frailty of his body. Caroline had spent long hours caring for John when he was sick, as well as making sure he had a proper edu-cation. John was a joy to teach, and he was quite gifted in science.

Caroline was a teacher, and her passion for teaching would ignite the classroom with gallant heroes and beautiful maidens from faraway lands, as history seemed to come alive and leap off the pages. There was no doubt in Caroline's mind that one day John would become a famous architect. As John grew, his health improved, and he was able to return to the school where Caroline loved to teach. Her family had built the town school just prior to Caroline graduating from the university. For two decades, that little school had been inspiring young minds to become their best.

Caroline didn't need the income; she had inherited her grandfather's lavish estate just before her twentieth birthday, and it was a grand inheritance; however, it came with a price. According to her grandfather's will, Caroline had to marry within one year of inheriting the estate, and she was expected to take her proper place in society. She wasn't afforded the luxury of meeting some handsome man on an enchanted evening and falling in love. Because of this stipulation, Caroline had to be married by her twenty-first birthday in order to receive her full inheritance.

Although Caroline's family had been the founding pillars of the community, she was quite shy in her youth. Caroline had attended all the social events, operas, and balls with the most glamorous gowns that money could afford; yet she had never been in love. Many times, she had dreamed of what it would be like to fall in love. She always envisioned it would happen on some starlit night—that she would meet her handsome prince. Their eyes would meet, and she would feel all warm and bubbly inside; he would ask her to dance, and once she was in his arms, she would know that he was the one. All throughout her high school and university years, she waited and dreamed such beautiful, lavish dreams, but still love did not come.

Caroline's father was an attorney, and he had introduced her to one of his business colleagues who was an engineer. The gentleman's name was William, a well-known businessman who was often referred to as being quite the ladies' man. When Caroline learned of William's reputation, she became very concerned and questioned her father's judgment in introducing her to such a man. Her father had said that it was only idle gossip, that William had a good head for business, and he would be a suitable companion for her. Hesitantly, she agreed to see William, and everything was neatly arranged as if it were a mere business contract.

Caroline was frustrated and angry with this ridiculous arrangement. What about her dreams and aspirations? Was she not entitled to have the same chance that every woman dreams of—to love and be loved? Why had her grandfather given her such a stipulation to inherit his fortune? The weight of it all just seemed unbearable. It felt so heartless and tragic that she thought her heart would burst with sadness and she sobbed bitterly. Perhaps she could refuse the inheritance and just pass it to her younger brother Edward, but what would everyone think of her?

Caroline knew deep in her heart she couldn't disgrace her family. No, she would just have to do the right thing as she always had. She would do what was expected and become the heiress that her grandfather had planned. As she dried her tears and pushed the thoughts from her mind, she tried to be optimistic. Perhaps her father was right, maybe it was a good arrangement, and perhaps she would learn to love William.

William and Caroline spent many hours together during their courtship. They dined in the most exquisite restaurants and attended every social event of the season. After a proper time of courtship, William asked for her hand and announced their engagement. Caroline's ring was ornate, abounding with beautiful smaller diamonds alongside the European-cut, three-karat diamond. The engagement party was the talk of the town. Everything almost seemed a blur; there had been one continuous party, event, or social gathering in the short six months they had been together, and now she was engaged to marry a man that she did not love. However, keeping with her grandfather's wishes, just two short months later, there was an elaborate wedding ceremony, and no expense was spared.

Caroline's glamorous dress was designed by the famous French designer, Jacques Doucet. Only the most exquisite handmade lace and beading were used to create his breathtaking masterpiece. After the wedding, the couple traveled to Europe and to Paris for a grand six-month honeymoon. Her wedding was everything a princess could have imagined—everything except love.

Caroline quickly assumed the role of heiress and handled her responsibilities quite well. Even though she worked tirelessly organizing charities, she was a very devoted wife to William. During the next sixteen years, Sarah and John were born, and Caroline became engrossed in being a wife and mother. The happiest moments in Caroline's life were spent with Sarah and John. They had a way of filling her heart with enormous, unending love and joy, something she would never know from her husband.

William's reputation had been quite correct— it wasn't mere rumors, he was definitely a ladies' man and spent an exorbitant amount of time at parties and away on business. It became abundantly clear that William had married Caroline for prestige, social status, and the family fortune. William was the type of man who would use anyone for gain. He was consumed with greed and power; he had a constant need to be in the limelight. In William's eyes, he was the best engineer, and he knew everything there was to know.

He spent no time with Caroline and the children unless it was to make a public appearance to make himself look good. When John was born, William became jealous because of the time Caroline spent with John due to his health; not that William had any love for Carolina, it was because she was unable to attend the social events and parties that inflated his ego. Her surreal marriage was one of duty and obligation.

One night William came home late after a party. He was angry and said he felt miserable. During the night, William became wrenched with pain and developed a fever. Caroline called for the doctor, and upon examination, the doctor told Caroline the grave news that William was desperately ill and must have surgery right away. William had developed some sort of infection in his abdomen, and his chances of survival were slim. Every preparation was made at the hospital that night, and the surgeon worked tirelessly for more than twelve hours in an attempt to eradicate the infection. However, it was to no avail; the infection was too great, and William did not survive the surgery.

It had been four years since William's death, and Caroline was ready to move on with life. Her children were the love of her life and gave her the only joy she had ever known. All too soon they would be leaving home to follow their dreams, and Caroline would be alone. There had always been a dream in Caroline's heart to find her soulmate and experience true love. She felt that she had been robbed of this privilege by her grandfather's will, and now she had the opportunity to finally pursue her dream.

In Caroline's heart, she longed to finally know the feeling of being held in the strong arms of a man that would love her forever. All the beautiful love stories that she had read about were only a dream to her. How her heart ached for the chance to feel that love. Caroline had often thought about the characteristics and qualities that she wanted in a man. He would be dashing, broad-shouldered, and have dreamy blue eyes, but he would also be compassionate, kind, caring, and gentle. The man of her dreams would love her unconditionally. and totally no matter her social status, someone she could laugh with, cry with, and share her life with. Caroline had spent many hours on the veranda pondering where she would ever meet such a man.

CHAPTER 2

ONE AFTERNOON, CAROLINE WAS WATERING the flowers on the veranda when she noticed a dark-haired man trimming hedges at the edge of the estate adjoining hers. He was only there for a short period of time, but something about his big, broad shoulders made her stop and take notice. He looked very confident in his abilities as he worked, yet he did not look like a mere gardener. Who was he, and why had she never noticed him before?

Early the next morning, Caroline went out on the veranda to have her tea, hoping to catch a glimpse of this intriguing man. Shortly afterward, he came across the side of the garden adjoining her estate and began his work. Quickly, she began working on her needlepoint and tried not to look as if she was watching him. Caroline just couldn't take her eyes off him; there was just something about the strength in those big, broad shoulders as he worked while the sun glistened on his gorgeous black hair. For several hours she sat there mesmerized, making very little progress on her needlework. Her handsome distraction was simply too tempting to resist watching.

That night Caroline was so excited she couldn't sleep; she felt as giddy as a schoolgirl, with a million questions racing through her mind as she lay there. Why had she never noticed him before? How long had he lived there? Where was he from? This mysterious man was a very handsome mystery, and one she hoped to solve. Over the next several days she returned to the veranda and pretended to busy herself tending the flowers; all the while she continued to watch him work, wondering if he had noticed her too.

Some days she would stand on the veranda and drink in the fragrance and the beauty of the majestic mountains that stood across from her estate, hoping to catch a glimpse of the dark-haired stranger. Caroline was intrigued by this dashing man, but how could she get him to notice her?

Finally, after several weeks had gone by, she could resist no longer; she just had to get his attention. Caroline decided to stroll through her lush flower garden, and from time to time she would stop and pretend to be weeding the flowers. Slowly, she worked her way closer to the edge of the property in his direction, and she stopped by the oak tree facing the gorgeous man that she was admiring. Finally, he noticed her; they exchanged smiles, and delight filled her heart. He put down his tools and walked toward her. Caroline was elated; he was actually coming to see her.

As her heart pounded with nervous anticipation, she felt a flood of emotions sweep over her in a way that she had never felt before. *What would he say? Had he seen her all along?* she thought nervously as she walked to the gazebo and sat down. When he reached the gazebo, a huge smile spread across her face as he walked over to meet her. Caroline felt her face blush when he approached. This dashing man had big, broad shoulders and gorgeous blue eyes, and he had the most dreamy-sounding voice she had ever heard as he introduced himself. His name was Peter; he was a sailor and was home on furlough.

After the formal introductions were made, she offered Peter a seat. Caroline was enchanted by the sound of Peter's captivating voice as he spoke. He told her that he had recently inherited the family home but did not get to enjoy it often due to duties as a sailor. There was an ample amount of work that he was trying to complete in the south garden. The previous gardener had been gone for quite some time, so there was lots of work to be done. Peter generously offered his assistance should she ever need any help on her estate.

She was lost in his dreamy, blue eyes and the delight that she felt simply being near him. Caroline smiled, thanked him kindly for his gracious offer, and invited Peter to come over for tea some afternoon. He smiled and politely accepted her invitation to do so.

Caroline would walk out every afternoon on the veranda just to watch Peter, looking at him with great anticipation, not knowing when he might decide to come calling on her. She had been admiring him for months, and it was too good to be true that she actually got to speak with him. A couple of days later, Peter knocked at the door, and Caroline asked him to have a seat on the veranda. There was a gentle breeze blowing that afternoon as she sat in one rocking chair and he sat across from her in the other one. They exchanged glances and smiles, and they discussed things that he had seen on his voyages.

Caroline was so intrigued by the sound of his beautiful voice and the exciting tales he told of his travels. She was so captivated by Peter that time almost seemed to stand still. For hours they sat engrossed in conversation, and when it was time to retire for the evening, Peter thanked her for a lovely time and promised to return. Caroline said good-night and watched him walk across the estate back to his home. He was the most enthralling man she had ever met; could this be the soul mate that she had longed for?

Could Peter be the man that she had prayed for and dreamed of? There was so much excitement in the air. The rush and the thrill of anticipation for his next arrival were so intense that Caroline could hardly sleep that night. Her heart and mind were still pondering the conversation of the evening, but more so, the charm of the dashing sailor that she had so quickly become fond of.

The next evening, promptly at dusk, Peter again knocked at the door. Caroline walked out on the veranda, and they sat for what seemed like hours. Again, they were engrossed in such stimulating conversation that Caroline hoped the night would never end. Peter, too, was becoming very fond of Caroline. He told Caroline that he was having to take an unexpected trip and would be gone for several days, but he would be back to see her as quickly as he arrived. When Peter stood to leave, Caroline arose to escort him down the veranda. Peter stopped, took Caroline in his arms, and kissed her gently on the cheek. Caroline was speechless; she felt flush as a huge rush of tingly emotion swept over her.

At that delicious moment in time, it didn't matter; it was just heavenly. He thanked her for a lovely evening and started out across the estate. The moment that Peter embraced Caroline, she could feel his strong arms, yet he was so gentle with his embrace. Caroline was overjoyed with these new feelings that she had not experienced before. Now, for the next three days, what would she do without Peter? The excitement of knowing that he was coming back to see her was enough to satisfy her heart and mind.

During those three days that seemed to drag on, Caroline kept herself busy, and from time to time, she would look out the window across the veranda and long to be in Peter's arms. How is it possible that she had developed such an attraction to him in such a short time? How she had dreamed of someone to love her deeply. Three days later, Peter came back from his trip and immediately came up the steps of the veranda and knocked on the door. Caroline knew instantly that it was Peter; she was so excited, like a kid in a candy store. She opened the door, and Peter took her in his arms, gave her a quick kiss on the cheek, and was off across the estate lawn.

Over the next three weeks, it was like a dream come true; they spent endless hours together. There were nights by the fire under the stars, and Peter would steal a kiss while they danced by the firelight. Sometimes they would walk hand in hand in the moonlight while Peter told of his adventures aboard the ship. Caroline loved listening to Peter talk, and she especially enjoyed the stories of the adventures on his voyages.

One night, as Caroline waited on the veranda for Peter, she thought about dancing in the moonlight. Oh, how she loved to dance, and she remembered all the lonely nights of dancing alone on the starlit veranda wishing for her handsome prince. That night, when Peter arrived, she asked him to dance with her. Peter gently took Caroline in his arms and held her close as they danced. With her cheek on Peter's chest, she could hear the sound of his heartbeat, and the sweet smell of his skin was intoxicating.

There was such strength in those loving arms, yet they held her so gently with tenderness and passion. Caroline felt so safe and secure, and an overwhelming surge of emotions that she had never known before swept over her. They danced for what seemed like an eternity under the celestial symphony. Peter smiled sweetly at Caroline and said, "You're like a school-girl." Neither of them wanted the enchanted evening to come to an end. It was like a fairy tale come true. The weeks passed all too quickly for Caroline, and Peter had to return to the duties of the ship.

CHAPTER 3

WITH A CRISP, COOL AUTUMN breeze, the beautiful, captivating summer had come to an end. Sarah watched excitedly that morning as her trunks were loaded into the carriage. She could hardly believe that in just a few hours she would begin her new life with classes at the university. Her list had been gone over very carefully several days before just to make certain that she had packed everything she would need, especially the latest fashion in ball gowns. Caroline and John were already seated in the carriage, waiting for Sarah to climb aboard for the journey.

John loved his sister and was not anxious for her to leave. The three of them were so close, and Sarah, wise beyond her years, had been such a comfort to

Caroline over the years. This new chapter of Sarah's life would be exciting and glamours, she would also miss her family very much, but she knew that her calling to become a teacher was awaiting her. The excitement of the day quickly overshadowed the sadness, and they talked happily on their journey toward Boston.

The university was only two hours away, and it was the same school that Caroline had attended, so it made her feel honored that Sarah had decided to attend the same university. Caroline was thankful there had been so much to do because it helped her pass the time and took her mind off the missing Peter so terribly. She tried to keep herself busy with the children. There was always an abundant supply of things to do. Still, one night, Caroline's heart yearned for Peter; it had been love at first sight; the first time she got to be in his arms, she knew immediately that she loved him.

Her constant fear was that she would lose him at sea, and she would never see him again. Caroline did not know how long Peter would be at sea or what dangers lay ahead. She only knew that this engulfing love that she had for him continued to grow daily. Every time she received a letter from Peter, she would feel the same exuberance and passion as the first night she was in his arms.

As the days went by, she tried to keep herself busy at school with lessons to grade and assignments to plan. Several months had gone by until one afternoon Caroline received a letter that Peter was coming home. She was so excited she would get to be in his loving arms once again. The day finally arrived when Peter's ship returned to port. and Caroline excitedly awaited Peter's visit. She had planned the most wonderful dinner and anxiously watched the clock.

Promptly at 5:30 p.m. Peter arrived, and when Caroline opened the door, her heart was pounding. All she wanted to do was be in his arms. Peter took her in his arms, and she held Peter so tightly she didn't want to let go. A huge rush of emotion and passion swept over her; it almost brought her to tears. Peter and Caroline had dinner with John, and later they retired to the parlor. Peter again took Caroline in his arms and kissed her so passionately. That long-awaited kiss had finally come, and his lips tasted so sweet. His strong arms held her so gently; Peter kissed her so passionately, yet the gentleness made her feel safe.

Never had she known a man with such passion, nor had she ever felt this passion for another man.

Each time Caroline saw Peter, her newfound love continued to flourish. One evening Peter told Caroline that he must again return to the ship. Caroline loved Peter, and she dreamed of him constantly; every time she closed her eyes, she could smell the scent of his skin.

Peter had been gone for about three months when Caroline received a letter saying that Peter had taken ill. He had been hospitalized, and his prognosis was grim. He had developed some sort of disease while working on a tropical island. Caroline's heart sank; it was gripped with fear and panic; what if he didn't survive? What if he never made it back home? Over and over again, it played out in her mind. What would she do? They had been together for seven months, and now would she lose him?

Her heart felt like it had been ripped from her chest, and tears poured down her cheeks in uncontrollable sobs. The last seven months had been so glorious, so carefree. Would it all end now? Was their time together really so brief? There were so many unanswered questions and fears. Caroline couldn't bear the thought of losing Peter. No, she would just have to be patient and pray. Every waking hour, her thoughts were of Peter. She tried not to let John see her discouragement and her pain. School kept her busy, so at least during the day, there wasn't time for grief, but the lonely nights and the evenings when she had no word, she could only pray for his survival.

Several weeks went by when, finally, there was word that he had been shipped home. He was still seriously ill, but was well enough to be out of the hospital. The disease had taken a toll on Peter's body, but he would recover. To Caroline, he was the most handsome man in the world, and she would have loved him no matter his fate. A week later she was able to see her beloved, and immediately she threw her arms around Peter; she was so elated that he had survived.

There simply weren't words good enough to describe her joy. She found no happier place on earth than with Peter, and she did not want to let go, but Peter needed his rest. She handed him a small gift and token of her love for him; he kissed her gently on the cheek and said goodnight.

Caroline was ecstatic; her prince charming was back home finally, hopefully for good. As the crisp, cool breeze of that February day blew across her face, she felt as if she would float away with sheer elation. Her heart was so at peace just knowing that he was home. She wondered how long it would be before she could see him again. A thousand thoughts raced through her mind with excitement, but for now she was just thrilled to have him home safe and sound. Over the next few weeks, they sent letters to each other, and even in his writing Caroline could feel his love and tenderness for her.

Peter was gradually returning to normal; although he had suffered some health problems, with medication, he would have a normal life. Caroline wouldn't have cared if he'd come home missing his arms. She loved him no matter what. Peter recovered quickly, and pretty soon life was back to normal. The love that Caroline had for Peter continued to grow abundantly, and the hours they spent together gave her happiness beyond her wildest imagination.

After making a full recovery, Peter returned to the duties of the ship, a day Caroline hoped would never come. She would continue praying and longing for his safe return. She soon realized that this immeasurable love that she had for Peter was so vast it was beyond words to describe.

Caroline continued to busy herself with the daily routines of teaching. Teaching had always been a passion for her, and she had dreamed of being a teacher as long as she could remember. When she was a child, she would spend endless hours playing school with her younger brother and cousin. Caroline knew deep in her heart that teaching had been her calling in life. Her passion for literature would ignite the classroom. She could tell stories endlessly with a newfound love each time she read them.

On that next Monday, Peter would be shipping out to sea, and she would have one more weekend with him before he left. As was their tradition, Peter came to dinner at Caroline's every Wednesday evening when he was home, promptly at 5:30 p.m. She wanted this Wednesday to be special and different from all the others they had had. Caroline cooked a feast; there was roast turkey with all the trimmings and his favorite desserts. Peter loved chocolate, so Caroline had made a decadent chocolate cake for him.

Every time Peter came to see her, she always greeted him at the door with open arms. The way Caroline felt when she wrapped her arms around Peter was the most exhilarating experience she could ever imagine. A huge rush of emotions would sweep over her with love and sheer joy; she could have hugged Peter forever. That particular evening the exuberance was intensified, and Carolyn had no idea why.

After dinner was over, Caroline and Peter retired to the parlor. Oh, how she enjoyed Peter's presence. She could have talked to him endlessly for hours or simply cuddled by the fire just to drink in the bliss of it all. This particular evening, Peter surprisingly began to talk about their future together. Caroline was shocked beyond words. She felt as if her heart would burst with happiness. Had her ears deceived her? Was Peter really talking about a life together in the future? Oh, how she had dreamed of the possibility; in all her lonely hours while Peter was away, she thought of nothing else.

Now Peter was actually discussing it. Caroline had never felt or known such happiness. Could this dream really come true? Peter couldn't have said anything to Caroline that would have made her any happier. Peter took Caroline in his arms and lovingly kissed her goodnight. The taste of Peter's sweet kiss lingered on her lips as she watched him ride across the estate.

Later that night, as Caroline tried to sleep, she couldn't help but think of Peter's words. It was all too deliciously wonderful to be true—how she had longed for this moment. Her life would be lived with Peter by her side. What adventures would await them? Would they travel to foreign and distant lands? The intoxicating joy was almost inconceivable, yet she finally managed to drift off to sleep with the taste of Peter's sweet kiss still lingering on her lips.

The next day dawned early with the magnificent smells of a beautiful spring day in May. There was excitement in the air; school would be out soon for the summer. Anxiously, Caroline had waited for the long summer nights when she could dance with Peter again under the stars again—the exuberance she felt just being wrapped in his arms, the swell sweet smell of his skin, and the gentleness of his touch. Carol felt so completely safe and loved by Peter, and her love continuously grew stronger. Such unimaginable love was almost too good to be true. She had never felt this way for any other man.

Peter had been out to sea for several months, and he would write to Caroline often. Caroline anxiously waited for his letters and his safe return. Before Peter shipped out, he offered Carolina a token of his love to keep her company while he was away. Peter had given Caroline his scarf. Peter's sweet scent was on the scarf, and she would hold it close on those lonely nights and dream about being in his arms. Caroline would put Peter's scarf on her pillow beside her each night, and she prayed for his safety and for God to watch over him, protect him, and bring him back safely to her.

CHAPTER 4

Unexpectedly, one afternoon, Caroline's son John became ill and was unable to see. The nearest doctor was over ten miles away, so quickly Caroline hitched the carriage and rushed John to the doctor. The roads outside of town were very rough and harsh to travel on. Caroline drove as fast as the horses could possibly carry them. As the thoughts raced through her mind, she tried to stay calm and keep a clear head. Her only concern was the safety of her child, and she feared she didn't have a moment to lose. As the carriage jolted and lurched on the bumpy road, John winced with pain and was quite uncomfortable. The sudden journey was uncomfortable for both man and beast. Both horses were in a lather by the time they reached their destination.

John's prognosis was uncertain, and the doctor said he had done all he could do. He said that John desperately needed to be in the hospital for fear that he might never regain his eyesight. Caroline and John would have to take the train to the nearest hospital, which was two hours away. Preparations were made for the trip, and the hospital would be expecting John's arrival. Caroline tried to make him as comfortable as possible on the train.

The smell of smoke permeated the air as passengers slowly boarded trains and found a seat. The minutes seemed to drag by endlessly while Caroline pondered everything the doctor had said. As she anxiously watched John, a million thoughts raced through her mind. *Would his blindness be permanent? Would he need surgery, and would they be able to cure him?* She refused to let her mind wonder into the land of what if. No, she had to keep a clear head and be sensible; she would be hopeful and pray for a miracle.

Finally, the train pulled into the station and jutted to a halt. A carriage was waiting to transport John to the hospital. Quickly, Caroline gathered her things, and with the help of the porter, she carefully placed John into the carriage. It was a short ride across town to the hospital, where the doctor was anxiously awaiting John's arrival. He was quickly taken to a room, and a fury of doctors and nurses came in and out of his room asking questions. The pungent smell of stitch and carbolic acid filled the air. At times, the odors were so intense they nearly took her breath.

John's doctor feared that John had suffered a stroke. For the next two weeks, there was very little sleep for Caroline in that small hospital room. The nurses kept coming into John's room at all hours of the night, and it was almost impossible to sleep in the chair. Several days went by with no improvement, and then a few days later he slowly began to improve. At the end of the second week, John was released from the hospital and was expected to make a full recovery. Thankfully it had not been a stroke; instead, he had suffered some sort of seizure.

As the weeks passed, life slowly returned to normal. Caroline had not been able to see Peter, and her heart longed for him every day. Some days she missed him so much it would bring her to tears. There was no other feeling on Earth that could compare to the way she felt when she was with Peter. The sheer joy of just a simple note from him was almost intoxicating. He wrote to Caroline several times a week, telling her of his voyages. The last one had been long and hard, and they had encountered numerous storms with much damage to the ship. Finally, after the repairs were made, the sailors were released to come home for a short furlough.

Friday afternoon, Peter came to see his beloved Caroline. She could hardly contain her excitement when she opened the door and Peter was there. In Peter's embrace, time seemed to stand still; there was no place in the world Caroline would rather be than in the arms of the man that she loved so dearly. They sat in the parlor and talked about how she loved his company again. Peter began talking about their future together and where they might live. Peter also had a surprise for Caroline; on one of his voyages, he found a little dog named Jack. Caroline was thrilled to welcome Jack to the family. She would have loved Peter, no matter what he brought home.

Peter's furlough had begun shortly before Father's Day, and Peter didn't seem himself somehow during that visit. He talked about being tired, and it was as if his thoughts were in a faraway place. Caroline tried not to make any notice of it, assuming he was just exhausted from his journey; still, she worried since his recent illness. No. She would just put it out of her mind, be happy, and enjoy the time that she had with him on his furlough. Peter was always happy to dance with Caroline on the veranda under the stars.

She remembered when they first met how many hours they spent looking into each other's eyes, dancing cheek to cheek, and how Peter would steal a kiss. The idea that she was going to get to spend the rest of her life with this wonderful man was just almost too good to be true. His two-week furlough had gone by so quickly, and it was almost as if it had only been a day. How Caroline dreaded the days that Peter had to return to sea.

Peter's ship left early that Monday morning, and he would be gone for three months to the South Pacific. Caroline wondered what grand new adventure Peter would meet on this voyage. He loved exploring uncharted islands in search of treasure. There was always some unique little gift he would find on the shore and bring to Caroline. He had given her a beautiful array of shells and exquisite tropical flowers. Life was so beautiful since Peter had come into her life. It was like a fairy tale—a dream come true. The idea of being able to share her life with Peter was almost breathtaking. Never had she known or ever imagined such happiness. Her life felt so complete, and for the first time she had finally experienced the love that she so desperately longed for.

Peter had been gone almost two months when one Saturday morning news came to Caroline that she would never forget. A messenger had brought a telegram to her door. Nervously, she opened the telegram, wondering what it was about. Caroline's first thoughts were of Sarah since she was away at the university. However, she quickly realized that it was about Peter. The telegram stated that Peter was missing and presumed he had been lost at sea. His ship had encountered a vicious storm, and there had been heavy casualties; most of the ship was destroyed, and his body had not been recovered.

Too weak to stand, Caroline fell to the floor in uncontrollable sobs; the most awful wave of horror and grief swept over her. How could this possibly have happened? She had been in his arms just a few weeks before, and now he was lost forever? It was unthinkable, unbearable; what would she do? She's cried until there were no tears left; her heart ached. How could he be gone? Her beloved Peter, the man she was going to spend her life with, how could he be gone?

The next few days seemed like a blur in Caroline's mind. It was like a horrible nightmare that refused to end. She felt so numb, emotionless, and very weak. She cried until there weren't tears left. How could she face the world again? How could she pick up all the pieces of her heart, which had felt like it had been ripped from her chest? The days turned to weeks, and Caroline continued to grieve for Peter. Thankfully, she had her children to give her comfort and to help occupy her mind. There wasn't a minute of the day that went by that she didn't grieve for the loss of her beloved. Why had it ended so tragically?

Caroline just merely existed; she just completed the routine rituals of the day and one day blended into the next. Why, why her? She had tried to be a good mother and teacher. She had always done the right thing. It was just so unfair. She felt like Peter was the only man she truly ever loved, and now he was gone, gone forever. She had never felt more passion and more alive than when she was with Peter, but now all that was gone.

CHAPTER 5

THE SUMMER HAD GONE BY far too quickly, and it was time to start the fall semester at school. Caroline welcomed the change because, at least at school, she was too busy to grieve for Peter. The school year started with many new faces and new challenges. Would there be enough supplies this year for the children? Would more teachers be sent to the valley to help with the overcrowding of her little school? John had made a full recovery and was doing quite well and was very anxious to return to class with his friends.

Sarah, too, was on her way back to class at the university, and by the end of the semester she would be in her final year of school. She was so excited to follow in her mother's footsteps and become a teacher.

Sarah had been a great source of strength for Caroline while she was grieving the loss of Peter. Sarah was wise beyond her years, and with her tenderness and compassion, Caroline knew that she would make a wonderful teacher. Caroline would miss her terribly; they had become so much closer, like best friends now that Sarah was older.

It had been almost six months since Peter's disappearance, and the authorities had given up all hope of ever recovering his body. The weeks and months seemed to drag by for Caroline, and all the energy that she had felt before was drained from her body. She felt numb most of the time, as if she were merely existing, just going through the motions from day to day. There wasn't a day that went by that she didn't grieve, and the waves of sorrow would wash over her with unimaginable heartache.

A constant sick, nauseating feeling gripped the pit of her stomach, and she could eat very little. Caroline felt like she was trapped in a horrible nightmare that wouldn't end, and she couldn't wake up. There were so many nights of endless tears until the wee hours of the morning. She would wrap Peter's scarf around her and cry herself to sleep. Time was supposed to heal all wounds, but in her case it didn't seem that way, and the heartache did not get any easier.

Thanksgiving was around the corner, and all the students at school were excited about the holiday break, anything to be out of school. John, however, didn't feel that way; he greatly enjoyed being at school. His thirst for knowledge was quite unusual for a boy of his age, and his favorite past times were his studies. Caroline hoped she could pry him away from his books to help her with the decorations, and perhaps they could bake desserts together.

She had hoped that all the festivities would make her feel like her old self again. Sarah would be coming home from the university, and the three of them would have a grand family Thanksgiving together. Although Caroline didn't feel like celebrating, she had to pull herself together for the children's sake. After all, the holidays were supposed to be a happy time with family and friends.

It hardly seemed like the turkey and pumpkin pie leftovers were finished until it was time to begin planning for the Christmas holiday. A Christmas Cotillion was to be held by the school board, and all the families in town were invited to come. The girls were ecstatic, each hoping to find the perfect ball gown, and anxiously awaited which boy would ask them to the dance. They talked excitedly as they transformed the ballroom into a Christmas winter wonderland. It was a happy time, but not for Caroline; all she could think about were the times that she and Peter had danced on the veranda under the stars and how being in his strong arms was almost breathtaking. Caroline wiped the tears from her eyes as she carried the decorations into the grand ballroom.

Sarah was home for the Christmas holiday and suggested that she and her mother were in need of a new dress in the latest fashions. The French silk ball gowns were all the rage at the university, and all the popular girls simply had to have one. Caroline agreed and hoped the festivities of the holidays would brighten her spirits; after all, at Christmas it would be six months since her terrible loss. She and the children busied themselves in endless hours of decorating for the holidays, and everything seemed almost perfect.

School would be out on the following Friday for the Christmas break. Caroline's house was elaborately decorated with Christmas trees, garland, holly, and anything that sparkled. She and the kids had baked dozens of cookies and cakes, and all the presents had been wrapped. Everything was ready for the holiday.

Caroline would have three whole weeks off from school to rest and relax from all her work. At seven o'clock that Friday night, the Christmas Cotillion was held in all its grandeur. John looked very dashing, Sarah was lovely, and Caroline looked exquisite. It was the first time that she had been dressed so elegantly without Peter.

There was a crisp winter chill in the air as they rode in the carriage. Other families were already arriving anxiously awaiting the evening's festivities. One by one, the girls and Sarah compared the latest fashions and blushed each time one was asked to dance. The night seemed absolutely perfect, except for the ache that continued in Caroline's heart. She tried to fight back the tears because the night reminded her so much of when she and Peter had gone to parties and dances. Caroline had hoped that the pain would have lessened by now. As she fought back the tears, she tried to enjoy the evening for the children's sake. Later, Caroline and the children arrived home exhausted, and she was emotionally drained. Snow had begun falling softly, which made it seem all the more like Christmas.

Thankfully, the Christmas break started the next day, but there was still so much to do preparing for a Christmas dinner and family get-together.

After she said good night to the kids, she retired to her room, and she held Peter Scarf and cried until she drifted off to sleep. Caroline tried to sleep the next day; after all, it was vacation, but it was no use; she was awake at 7:30 a.m. She got up, got dressed, and busied herself making breakfast for the kids. She went over to the parlor and opened the curtains just to see how much it had snowed during the night.

Everything looked beautiful; it looked like a big, white, fluffy blanket had tucked everything in for the winter. In her excitement of looking at snow, Caroline didn't think about Peter's estate being across the way. A huge rush of emotions engulfed her all at once. How many days had she stood at that window waiting for Peter to come home? Since his disappearance, she had no desire to go into the parlor or even close to that window. The huge rush of emotion was so strong it was almost sickening, and she felt weak.

Quickly, she left the parlor and tried to put it out of her mind. "Poor Peter, oh my love, Peter, why did this have to happen? Why?" she said, and then she broke into uncontrollable sobs. Caroline tried not to let her mind wander, but at that moment, the emotions of longing for Peter and all they had dreamed about together were just so overwhelming that she fell to the floor and cried until she had no tears left.

Later that evening, there was to be a family Christmas party. Caroline finally managed to pull herself together. Her red, swollen eyes and her tear-streaked face would need much attention if she were to look her best for the evening. Somehow she managed to conceal the events of her morning and prepared the evening meal. It wasn't too long after she and Sarah were in the kitchen that the room became filled with laughter. Sarah was excited because she now had a beau, and his name was Theodore. His parents were quite wealthy, and they were a prominent family in the community.

Caroline had hoped that Sarah would wait until after she had graduated from the university and then consider finding a beau. Caroline knew all too well the heartbreak of being separated from the man that you love.

The days of Christmas vacation went swiftly by, and it was almost Christmas. In just two more days, it would be Christmas. Caroline's mind wandered back to her first Christmas with Peter and the gifts she had given him. She tried desperately not to let her mind go there, but somehow she couldn't stop it. She still had last-minute purchases to make and gifts to wrap. Also, there was one final party to attend, and hopefully that would keep her mind well occupied.

Finally, Christmas Eve arrived, and Caroline was painting in the study; it was almost time for bed. Painting always helped Caroline relax, and she loved it. She loved painting almost as much as she did dancing. She looked at the clock on the wall as it chimed ten o'clock, and suddenly, there was a knock at the door. *Who could it be at this hour?* Caroline's mind pondered the possibilities of who it could be; she wasn't expecting company. *Was someone ill?* Nervously, Caroline went to the door and opened it. There stood Peter in the doorway, smiling. Shock, almost panic, and then elation all swept over Caroline like a flood. She stood there, almost holding her breath, as if he would disappear.

Immediately, Caroline grabbed Peter and held him as tightly as she possibly could. Tears were streaming down her face; she was almost hysterical with joy. At that delicious moment in time, there were no words, no questions, nothing. She couldn't have spoken even if she'd wanted to, for at that glorious moment, all she could do was stand there and be held in the strong arms of the man that she loved so dearly.

Never had Caroline experienced such joy and happiness. It was simply beyond words. Peter stood there and gently stroked her hair and smiled so lovingly at her. Time seemed to stand still as she was engulfed in passion and euphoria, while every ounce of her body clung to Peter with all her might. Her great love for Peter was truly overwhelming.

When Caroline was finally able to compose herself, they walked into the parlor. She couldn't let go of Peter, not even for a second. When at last she was able to speak, all the thoughts rushed to her at once. She felt like it was a beautiful dream, too good to be true. Peter smiled, and he said, "It's not a dream. I'm here." They embraced and held each other; there would be plenty of times to answer questions about what had happened. For now, all she wanted to do was hold him and never let go. Caroline was so excited that her body shook uncontrollably from the inside out.

Peter held her so tenderly, and as he took her in his loving arms, he kissed her passionately. Oh, how she had missed the sweet taste of his lips. The pain and the agony she had felt during those months were over, and it all seemed to just melt away in his arms. Peter told Caroline he was so sorry that he had caused her so much pain, but all the pain that Caroline had felt evaporated the minute she was with him.

Peter had brought gifts for Caroline and the children; he had left them on the table in the parlor. The only gift Caroline had ever wanted was Peter. When she finally had to kiss him good night, she hated to see him go, but the hour was getting late. Caroline was still so excited that her entire body shook from the inside out; never had she experienced such happiness. Her beloved Peter was finally home.

CHAPTER 6

IT HAD BEEN THREE GLORIOUS weeks since Peter had returned home, and Caroline could not be happier. The happiness that she felt inside was indescribable compared to the six months of agony that she had felt fearing that Peter had drowned in the sea. After just one evening with him, all the pain and the heartache were simply erased. The experience Peter had gone through was quite traumatic. She hadn't learned the details of the voyage. but she was sure there would be plenty of time to learn what had happened. For now, just having him home safe and sound was more than enough for her. Although they hadn't seen each other during those three weeks, they continued to send messages.

Caroline knew that he needed his rest, and she joyously prayed for his healing and his strength.

Just to know that Peter was resting was enough to satisfy her mind. She knew that she could simply look across the estate and feel confident that Peter was recuperating safely at home. Caroline had so much to do, so many plans to make, happy plans. It was such a wonderful change to feel happy again and dream of being held so securely in the arms of the man that she loved so passionately. Love, this indescribable, engulfing love that she felt for Peter was so strong that it almost brought her to tears.

Several weeks had gone by, but Caroline still had not seen Peter. One evening, she received a letter from Peter; it was scented with his cologne, and the smell permeated the room. Caroline went to the parlor and sat down to read Peter's letter. Caroline knew that Peter loved her deeply; there was no question in her mind or her heart as to his feelings for her. She opened the envelope and read…

My dearest love Caroline,

You have been so patient and kind all these months since I've returned from that terrible accident. Our ship was somewhere around the coast of Africa; there was a terrible storm, and the ship was tossed like a rag doll on the sea. The men feared for their lives on that dark, dreary, stormy night. The breakers crashed on the starboard side of the ship, ripping at the sails; the waves were so violent we feared the ship would be ripped apart. There was no safe place aboard the ship to escape the violent storm, and the crew worked tirelessly for hours just to keep the ship afloat. Then, just before dawn, the ship was blown violently into the cliffs, and the jagged rocks ripped apart the hull of the ship. That was the last time I ever saw my crewmen again, and I do not know if anyone else survived that night. Clinging to a broken piece of the ship, I was knocked unconscious by flying debris. All I know is that when I awoke, I was on the beach, and the sun was shining brightly with the gentle breeze and a beautiful blue sky, as if it had all been a dream. I tried to move, but my leg had been injured. Thankfully it wasn't broken, and I was quite lucky to be alive. It was quite difficult the first few days because I was unable to walk and weak from hunger. Every day was a struggle to survive; luckily some of the supplies aboard the ship were washed ashore as well. During the first few weeks, I stayed on the shore hoping for rescue, but as the weeks passed and my leg healed, I gave up all hope of a search party coming to find me. I had no idea how long I would be on that island or even its exact location. When I was well enough, I tried to explore as much as possible, hoping to find other people that could help me. It was to no avail; the island was completely deserted other than the wildlife. I made a camp not far from shore that gave me shelter during the day, and it was close enough to see if a ship was coming. The days, the nights, and the weeks all seem to *blur* together in one long day. The isolation from the outside world was almost unbearable.

Even though there was an abundant supply of fruit and fish on the island, there was still the constant fear of survival. My thoughts were of you and how badly I wanted to be on the veranda holding you under the stars. I knew your heart was broken, not knowing that I was alive, and the sheer thought of you being so brokenhearted was almost more than I could bear. Your great love for me gave me the strength and the reason to hope that one day I would be rescued and we would be together once more. My love for you, although I've never spoken to you of it, continues to grow. I wept many nights knowing that you were brokenhearted.

Since the boat was destroyed, they presumed we were all dead. After several months had passed, I had almost given up all hope of ever being rescued, and then late one evening, just before dusk, a ship was on the horizon. At first, I thought it was a mirage because of all the lonely days I waited for a ship to come. After realizing that it was not a dream, I quickly built a fire, and eventually that night, I was rescued. All my thoughts were of you, my dear, sweet Caroline, and all of my hopes became anew.

I once again would be able to
hold you in my arms.

With all my love,
Peter

The next day, she knew that Peter was going to be busy, and she hoped she would see him afterward. She waited all Christmas Day and into the evening, but Peter did not come. Caroline waited several more days, and at one point she even sent a note to Peter asking him to come to dinner, but he sent his regret that he wouldn't be able to make it. Puzzled and confused, Caroline didn't know what to say or to think. She tried to tell herself that he was just exhausted from being on the island for so long and just needed time to recover. Days went by, and she sent letters and invitations to Peter. He would reply simply, saying he was unable to make it.

Weeks went by and Peter still never came, so one Sunday evening, she decided to make his favorite dessert and take it to him. Peter came out into the yard and stood near her carriage. Caroline got down and went to Peter, happy to see him and excited that he was really there. Peter offered her his hand, but this time something seemed different about Peter.

He was hesitant and standoffish. Caroline tried to embrace Peter, and she tried to ignore any negative emotions. Peter began to talk about making a fresh start with his life.

He explained he had so much work to do on his estate, things that he had neglected and just simply had to be done. Naturally, since he and Caroline had discussed their future together before the accident, Caroline assumed that he was talking about them being together, so she agreed that yes, a fresh start would be wonderful and they would find a new place to live.

They talked and embraced for a while, and Caroline told Peter that no matter where they went or what they did, she would love him no matter what. Caroline would follow Peter to the ends of the earth. Her love was so great for him. Peter knew of Caroline's great love, and he knew that that love continued to grow every day. Peter looked very distant and tired. He thanked her for the dessert and gently kissed her on the cheek. Caroline climbed into her carriage and went home.

Several weeks went by, and from time to time, Caroline would receive a note from Peter. This was quite usual considering she had spent every waking hour with Peter when he was home on furlough, and now Peter had changed. He was so different. Every day that went by, Caroline tried to convince herself that it was just because of his accident, and nothing had really changed. After all, how could he have taken her in his arms so lovingly on Christmas Eve with all the joy and love they shared. They both had been enraptured to be together once more that night. Now how could that have possibly changed?

Caroline forced the thoughts out of her mind, but somehow Peter was different, and he was becoming increasingly more distant every day. Caroline had experienced such a vast array of emotions, from sheer joy, pleasure, and happiness to unbearable horror and agony when she thought he was lost for good. Then such elation and happiness when he was found and returned home once again. With the constant bewilderment as to why Peter had become so distant one Saturday afternoon, Caroline could take it no longer.

With all her heart had endured, it just didn't make any sense, so she wrote Peter a letter explaining her feelings and telling Peter she did not understand what was wrong. She felt like she was being punished for something but had no idea what. Caroline was second-guessing herself, thinking perhaps maybe she shouldn't have said anything at all, but shortly thereafter, Peter's reply came.

> My dearest one, I'm sorry you feel like you're being punished. I do not mean for that to be so. You, my love, have done nothing wrong. I'm afraid the trauma that I received during the shipwreck and that six months of isolation were just too much. Is it not possible for me to be in a relationship.
>
> Peter

Caroline felt as if she were going to choke, and her heart felt like it was being ripped from her chest once again. With her hands shaking and tears streaming down her face, she held Peter's letter and screamed, "No, no, no!" She kept saying it over and over again. "How could this be? Fate was too cruel to fall in love with a man to lose him not once but twice."

Caroline cried for hours, and the hours turned to days. Still, she sobbed, and her heartache was unbearable. It was too painful to even imagine. All her hopes and dreams had been dashed not once but twice, and it was much worse this time because Peter was very much alive and how she longed to be by his side. How she longed to be in his arms and to feel his embrace. What had it all been for? Why did this happen? It was just too unimaginable, and the tears flowed like rivers. The pain was so excruciating at times that it was almost crippling.

Caroline wondered if she would ever be able to pull herself together. It was the most unthinkable, unimaginable thing she could think of. What began as a beautiful, enchanting dream became a heartache. The pain was so nauseating Caroline wept until she could weep no more; every day was a struggle. The emotion was so overwhelming most days that she couldn't eat.

Caroline still kept Peter's scarf on her bed, and she would pray for Peter's recovery, because never had she known such love for any other man. She felt quite sure she never would again. Caroline told herself if she couldn't have Peter, then she would just be alone, but the pain, the loneliness, and the grief that she felt for Peter just continued to grow. Caroline struggled every day for motivation to even get out of bed. She felt there was nothing anymore except her children and her faith in God.

Caroline forced herself to stay in a routine of teaching and taking care of things. Her friends tried to offer support, and finally one day a friend told her it was time to be realistic and move on with her life and just accept that Peter's gone. Caroline hesitated at first; no, she couldn't be unfaithful to Peter, not the man that she had loved more than words could express. How could she dare not give him time and hope that he would recuperate? If she truly loved him, she would wait forever; she would argue, "Love is patient, and love is kind." She was just determined to be patient and kind and continue loving Peter.

Months went by, and Caroline simply pretended that everything was fine, and it was as if Peter was still out at sea and she would just continue as she had in the times past. In her mind, nothing had changed, and she would remain faithful to her true love. After months had passed, Caroline began to realize that something had changed and Peter wasn't the same man that she knew. She began to think that perhaps she wasn't being realistic and maybe it was best for her health to just try and move on with her life. So that day Caroline told herself that the Peter that she knew and loved was lost at sea, and he never came home. The Peter that she had known had died in the shipwreck.

Caroline's friends tried to be nice. They planned parties, and all the eligible, available men would attend; unfortunately, this only made Caroline miss Peter that much more. She didn't know if there would ever be way a to say goodbye to Peter. In her heart, she dreamed that one day Peter would be well enough to return to her loving arms.

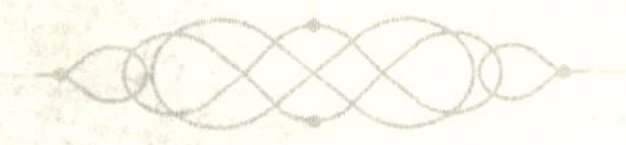

ABOUT THE AUTHOR

Tamella White is a mother of five children, an educator, and a hopeless romantic with a passion for writing. Her favorite time period is the late 1800s, with all its elegance and fashions, which thus inspires her writing.